ALL LISBON
AND ITS SURROUNDINGS

Text by XAVIER COSTA CLAVELL

Photographs, lay-out and reproduction, entirely designed and created by the Technical Department of EDITORIAL ESCUDO DE ORO, S.A.

Rights of total or partial reproduction and translation reserved.

Copyright of this edition for photographs and text: © EDITORIAL ESCUDO DE ORO, S.A.

3th Edition, June 1981

I.S.B.N. 84-378-0268-7

Spanish	84-378-0466-3
French	84-378-0467-1
English	84-378-0468-X
German	84-378-0469-8

Dep. Legal B. 16870-XXIV

Distributor for Portugal: LINO E FERREIRA, LDA.
Rua do Almada, 57-59 - Rua José Falcão, 86-96. Telephones: 29445 - 29446 - 22117 -22118
PORTO - PORTUGAL

 **escudo de oro, s.a.** Palaudarias, 26 - Barcelona, 4 - Spain
Impreso en España - Printed in Spain
F.I.S.A. Palaudarias, 26 - Barcelona-4

An old engraving of Lisbon on show in the City Museum.

LISBON, THE MUCH PRAISED CITY...

Long before Lisbon attained the status of Roman municipality in the I century A.D., both Phoenicians and Carthaginians had made their way there. Sited in a truly privileged location on hills and on the banks of the Tagus, whose magnificent estuary it overlooks, the city was inhabited at least 2.500 years before the birth of Christ, as shown by Bronze Age remains found around the lovely areas where Lisbon now stands. The great Portuguese poet of the «saudade», Teixeira de Pascoaes, described in enamoured verse the unique situation of the evocative capital of Portugal:

Surge Lisboa, branca, ao pé do Tejo azul;
A Lisboa das naus,
Construída em marfim, sobre colinas de oiro.
Vede o imenso estuário... (é sonho ou realidade?)
Sob um Azul divino a desfolhar-se em asas!

Tiles commemorating the capture of Lisbon.

The Visigothic walls of the old city and the vantage point and church of Santa Luzia.

Figueira Square, viewed from St. George's Castle.

Lisbon, the Atlantic city beloved of poets, deserved the honour of immortal Camões' inventing the charming legend that it had been founded by Ulysses, no less.

After its historic circumnavigation directed by the Romans, — who first called it *Olisipo* and later, *Felicitas Julia,* — Lisbon was occupied by Aluns, Suevians, Visigoths and Arabs, being conquered by the Christian hosts of Afonso Henriques, the first Portuguese king, in the year 1147.

From that moment on, the city on the Tagus became larger and acquired a new appearance, going beyond the confines of its walled precinct. Lisbon became the capital of the kingdom of Portugal in the XIII century, and instigated a period of splendour that reached its zenith when, at the beginning of the discoveries on the other side of the Atlantic and with the discovery of Brazil and the trade route to the Indies, it became the most important port in the world.

In 1755, Lisbon lived through tragic moments when it was destroyed by a colossal earthquake. The mediaeval part of Lisbon was reduced to the limits of the attractive Alfama district. The city itself was rebuilt under the dynamic and intelligent direction of the Marquis de Pombal, and a new Lisbon was created in geometrical style. The lines established by Pombal largely determined the subsequent growth of this lovely city, and Lisbon, without losing its charming characteristic aspect, became the great modern city it is today.

A statue of Don José I and the archway on the Rua Augusta.

THE CITY

Lisbon, this *eighth wonder, the greatest in Christendom, this outstanding city, famous and most noble —* according to the laudatory description made of it by Tirso de Molina in *El Burlador de Sevilla —*, stretches out, blue and silver, on the banks of the Atlantic, whose sea routes it formerly controlled and for which it is now an obligatory stopping place.

The oldest part of the city lies in terraces at the foot of St. George's Castle and was the original nucleus of the city. When the walled precinct stubbornly defended by the Moslems was stormed by Christian troops in 1147, the first real enlarging of Lisbon began, with the picturesque mediaeval district of Alfama moving towards the river Tagus. This ancient quarter surrounding the castle, seat of the Portuguese kings for four centuries, overlooks the two Lisbons that are now intermingled — the Lisbon of today and yesterday. Gradually, the centre of gravity of the city has moved downwards, increasingly nearer to the Tagus. The devastating earthquake of 1755 interrupted Lisbon's charmingly anarchical growth and brought about the subsequent city planning by the Marquis de Pombal, thus modernizing the city's appearance. Nevertheless, some delightful urban relics of the past have survived, apart from the Alfama and the Bairro Alto; there are others with such a marked personality as the Mouraria area, the Madragoa and the São Cristóvão district, along whose charming little streets are

5

A view of the Comércio Square or Terreiro do Paço.

old palaces and attractive churches, making a lively scene, colourful and vivacious, but tinged with melancholy.

A particularly interesting area of the city in its structure and human appeal is the district known as «Baixa» or the part lying between the popular squares of Rossio and Comércio whose main roadway is the Rua Augusta. Here are the banks and big businesses. There are also many bars, and tourists stroll about in a leisurely fashion, looking here and there, at every hour of the day.

After looking in fascination at the river and admiring the architectural harmony of the Comércio Square, which has the most balanced proportions and is the largest in Europe, facing the Tagus with the equestrian statue of José I in the centre, designed by

Machado de Castro — people return to the city centre and sit on the busy terraces of the typical cafés in Rossio.

A part of the city with a well-defined personality is the so-called «Chiado» which includes the *largo* of this name, the *largo* named after Camões, where the statue of the author of *Os Lusíadas* stands, designed by Victor Bastos erected in 1867, the Rua do Carmo and the Rua Garret, named after the Portuguese author of this inspiring line:

A pátria é pátria já; nós somos homens!

These last two streets — perhaps the most traditionally elegant in Lisbon — are filled with luxury shops, prestigious book shops, tea rooms and a café

famous for its literary and artistic gatherings — «A
Brasileira». Fashion in Portugal emanates from the luxurious shop windows of the Rua Garret which is also
a centre for brilliant literary activity and social chit-
chat.

«O Chiado», with its many cake shops, florists and
coffee sellers, is the centre of fashionable life in
Lisbon, frequented by many people who are in the
public eye, and also by those who would like to be.
There are three establishments which are by way of
being the nerve centres of social life in Lisbon; «A
Brasileira» where art, literature and politics are
discussed, the «Turf», and the «Grémio Literário»,
places for meetings connected with high finance, the
aristocracy, and eminent personalities from the world
of Portuguese letters. Formerly, a select group of

poets and writers calling themselves «Os vencidos da
vida», used to meet in the «Chiado» together with Eça
de Queiroz.

The monument to the Restorers, an obelisk thirty
metres high rises up beside the station of Rossio, opposite the Foz Palace, the statue was built in 1882 to
commemorate the 1640 revolution and Portuguese independence, and it is here where the lovely Avenida
da Liberdade begins, Lisbon's main thoroughfare two
kilometres long leading to the beautiful Edward VII
park. The Avenida da Liberdade, on whose highest
point stands the bronze statue of the Marquis de
Pombal, stretches out, flanked by cinemas, theatres,
and hotels.

In Lisbon there still remains the enchantment of the
typical districts of Alfama, with its labyrinthine and

The façade of the church of Our Lady da Conceição.

The archway on the Rua Augusta leading to the Comércio Square.

delightful old urban structure, and the Bairro Alto, the original setting for old folklore reminiscences with many places where *fados* are sung and also where quite a few of Lisbon's daily papers at present have their offices. To walk along these enchanting streets is to appreciate the spiritual quality and the soul of old Lisbon, filled with mystery and poetry, picturesqueness and nostalgia.

The gardens of Lisbon deserve a paragraph of their own, and among the most outstanding of these is the vast Botanical Garden, one of the loveliest in Europe, founded in 1875, with gigantic green houses and more than twenty thousand exotic plants; the magnificent Parque Florestal de Monsanto from whose vantage points there is a fine view dominated by the Tagus; the fabulous Estufa Fria, the gardens of Santa Catarina, São Pedro de Alcântara, the Príncipe Real, the Praça da Alegria, Campo Grande, Campo de Ourique, Mata de Benfica, Ajuda, the Garden da Estrela, and the Zoological Garden...

But possibly Lisbon's greatest charm of the many varied ones it possesses is that of its people, with their jovial nature and polite manners, their fine sensibility and sense of humour, their patriotic spirit and deep-rooted friendliness, their natural aristocratic bearing and melodious way of speaking. Among the inhabitants of Lisbon, one feels to be completely surrounded by friends.

The façade of Lisbon cathedral.

The truth is that there is no exaggeration in the popular Portuguese saying: *Quem não viu Lisboa não viu coisa boa* («He who has not seen Lisbon hasn't seen anything worth while»). Cardoso Martha dedicated some fine melancholy verses to the city:

> *Princesa do Sol-Pôr, que se reclina*
> *sob o dossel dum céu esbraseado*
> *beija-lhe os pés o Tejo, deslumbrado*
> *da sua imperial graça latina.*

From the proud balconies overhanging the Tagus, a fine view of the estuary can be seen from the Comércio Square and at night in the moonlight it becomes an even more fabulous sight, like some fantastic scene from *A Thousand and One Nights.*

THE CATHEDRAL

This is one of Lisbon's most ancient monuments. The popular *Sé,* built during the reigns of Afonso Henriques and Sancho I, was reconstructed at different periods after having been partially destroyed by various earth tremours. Nevertheless, its original Romanesque construction still preserves much of its purity of style. Apparently, the Englishman, Gilbert Hastings, who was to be the first bishop of Lisbon, was one of the most active promotors of the erection of Lisbon cathedral.

The cloister and chapel of Joanes are of Gothic inspiration. Outstanding for their beauty are the Romanesque windows on the façade and the vaults in the same style over the nave, also the Sacristy, the grave stones — especially the one convering the tomb of Lopo Fernandes Pacheco —, the richly adorned Romanesque railing closing off one of the chapels in the decorative Gothic cloister, the transept and the ambulatorium, with its tumuli and chapels in the apses.

The structure of the cathedral has rather the look of a mediaeval fortress. Partially destroyed by the 1755 earthquake, its rebuilding was not completed until 1940. Its lovely outline stands out elegantly not far from the curious Casa dos Bicos and the church of Santo António, close to the Tagus.

The cathedral cloister.

The Charola chapel and tomb of Lopo Fernandes Pacheco.

◁ *The façade of the church of Santo António.*

The interior of the Santo António Museum and a statue of Santo António, the patron saint of Lisbon.

THE CHURCH OF SANTO ANTÓNIO

This church stands close by the cathedral, in the same place as the Senate used to be; built under the direction of the architect Mateus Vicente, it belongs to the Municipal Chamber.

The church was built in honour of the most popular and venerated saint in the city and its crypt is still preserved, now known as the Santo António Museum, where, according to tradition Fernando de Bulhões was born who was later to die in Padua being

The façade of the popular Casa dos Bicos.

canonized as Saint Anthony. Legend has it that when the saint died, all the bells of Lisbon spontaneously tolled for the dead man.

When the original church of Santo António was destroyed by an earthquake, it was immediately rebuilt, the expenses being defrayed by donations and alms given by the people of Lisbon to children who went collecting from door to door.

The work on the construction of the new church of Santo António was under the direction of Mateus Vicente, the architect who also built the Basílica da Estrela in Lisbon and the Queluz Palace.

The crypt has still been preserved where, according to tradition, Santo António was born on August 15th 1195. The venerated Portuguese saint was, it appears, the son of Fernando de Bulhões and Teresa Taveira and was baptized in this place.

THE CASA DOS BICOS

Also known as the Casa dos Diamantes, this unusual building was constructed by Don Bras, son of the famous don Afonso de Alburquerque, who was Governor of Portuguese India in the XVI century. The building is in Renaissance style with points as the predominating adornment on the façade.

The Casa dos Bicos was partially destroyed by the 1755 earthquake and since then only two storeys remain of the original four storeyed building. The façade is reminiscent of those on the «Casa de los

A partial view and St. George's Castle.

Picos» in Segovia, and the «Pallazo dei Diamanti» in Ferrara.

St. GEORGE'S CASTLE

Sited on the highest hill in the Tagus estuary, from this privileged spot the whole of the Lisbon area can be overlooked and the castle, with its romantic architectural impact, can be seen from any part of the city.

St. George's Castle was built before the foundation of the Portuguese nationality and is Lisbon's most ancient monument. A royal residence from the time of Afonso Henriques to the reign of Manuel I, it still preserves the walls surrounding the fortress and the gateway where Martim Moniz lost his life bravely fighting against the Arabs who were defending the proud castle, near to which is the church of Santa Cruz, built on the site of a former mosque.

Beside the castle is the statue of St. George at whose service there was always a horse chosen from among the best in the kingdom, since king don Sancho bequeathed the Saint his when he died.

The terraces and towers of this imposing mediaeval fortress — beautifully reconstructed in 1947, to commemorate the eight centuries after the Christian conquest of Lisbon —, make a fine vantage point from which to see the magnificent panoramic view with the Tagus and the whole city stretching out beneath: a real feast for the eyes.

Two details of St. George's Castle and the façade of one of the oldest houses in Lisbon, situated in the Largo do Menino de Deus.

Partial view of the city with the Tagus in the background.

THE TAGUS

The river is the life line of Lisbon. It gave birth to the Portuguese capital, nurtured it and goes on giving it sustenance. Lisbon is wholly identified with the Tagus. *Cidade-río* (river-city) Mário Dias Ramos aptly named it in the title to a poem in his work *Morfogenia.* The river appears on every side, as though ensnared by the lovely city in a passionate and ceaseless love affair, giving itself completely and yet demanding to be perpetually contemplated by the loved one in return.

The city lies alongside the river for some 14 or 15 kilometres. Until the cyclopean bridge that now bears the name «April 25th» was built — a true feat of modern engineering — the Tagus divided the city into two parts whose only means of communication was by boat. Today the bridge has shortened the distance between both banks considerably and the river can be crossed by car in no time. Nevertheless, it is still a fine impressive tourist trip to cross the Tagus in a pleasure boat. Once you are in the middle of the river, surrounded by the grandiose estuary, the waters of the river will be confused with those of the sea and it will be almost impossible to find where the mouth of the river is situated.

The vast mirror of the waters with the image of city reflected in it dazzles the onlooker. Anyone who has looked at and enjoyed the privilage of seeing with the eyes of the soul the limitless and shimmering surface of the estuary will have had one of the most memorable experiences that human sensibility can

*A night time view of the «April 25th» bridge over the
Tagus.*

appreciate. The unique beauty of the river inspired
António Ferreira, in the XVI century, to write these
emotive verses:

> *Tejo triunfador do claro Oriente,*
> *Que Nilo e Ganges por senhor conhecem;*
> *Tejo que areias de ouro, onde florecem*
> *Pales, Pomona, e Flora eternamente;*
> *Tu levas, onde eu fico, tua corrente.*
> *Se saudosas lágrimas merecem*
> *(Pois tanto com elas tuas águas crecem)*
> *Piedade, em ti as recolhe brandamente...*

Lisbon and the Tagus are inextricably associated, the
city and the river forming a harmonious whole, ap-
pearing to have been made for one another. The
Tagus is the beautiful wide window through which
Lisbon looks onto the Atlantic with graceful majesty.
As the Portuguese capital is situated on one of the
longest and most delightful estuaries in the world,
this privileged position made it into an extremely important port throughout its illustrious and eventful
history; this importance was duly recognized by the
Emperor Charles I of Spain and V of the Holy Roman
Empire when he exclaimed on one occasion: «If I
were king of Lisbon I would be king of the world».
The charm of the Tagus caused Camilo Castelo Branco to write:

> *À noite, à beira do Tejo, (...)*
> *nascia a vida encantada...*

The Tagus is intimately linked with the history and the daily life of Portugal. It is a reflection of the myth and also of the human characteristics of the people of Lisbon. This is how the poet Armindo Rodrigues sees it:

Nas tardes dos domingos em que o sol
tem um brilho mais nítido e mais quente
e os cafés estão cheios de uma gente
burguesa, tola, amargurada e mole,
busco a beira do Tejo transparente.

Aos altos cumes de eternidade
aqui ergueu Camões a glória brava
da pátria que um eclipse já espreitava,
e morreu de pobreza e da saudade
do amor impossível que o queimava...

THE CHURCH OF SÃO VICENTE DE FORA

This is one of the churches in which the balanced style of the Portuguese Renaissance is most faithfully

Several views of the picturesque Feira da Ladra.

Façade of the church of São Vicente de Fora and a statue of this popular saint from Lisbon.

A panoramic view of the National Mausoleum. ▷

reflected. The church of São Vicente, whose construction was directed by the Italian architect Terzi, has a façade with three porticoes and two towers of elegant measured design and evident Roman influence.

The church was built in honour of a saint who formerly enjoyed great popularity in Lisbon. A delightful legend states that in 1173, a boat without oars or oarsmen ran aground in one of ramifications of the Tagus, guided by a pair of crows, and in it was the body of St. Vincent who had been tortured by the Arabs in the lands of Algarve. After the saint's remains had been taken to a safe place, the two crows flew towards Lisbon cathedral and made their nest in one of its towers.

The Don José Chamber and silver objects dating from the XVIII century in the Museum of Decorative Arts.

THE MUSEUM OF DECORATIVE ARTS

Belonging to the Ricardo Espírito Santo Foundation, the Museum is installed in a fine XVII century palace at number 90 on the calle de São Tomé. This palace, one of the oldest in Lisbon, belonged to the counts of Arnoso.

The content of the Museum of Decorative Arts is made up of interesting collections of period furniture, valuable tapestries, ceramic objects, metal ornaments, and old engravings.

The inside of the palace, still preserving its attractive original structure, and the tastefully decorated rooms, make this Museum a particularly evocative place to visit.

Another view of the Museum of Decorative Arts. ▷

Four views of the attractive Alfama district and four views of the popular festivity of Santo António.

A close-up of the Rua Augusta.

Two daytime views of the Rossio Square, and a night time view of the same area.

THE ALFAMA DISTRICT

This ancient quarter whose history goes back to the period of Visigothic domination, contains the most picturesque of buildings. The Alfama begins at the foot of St. George's Castle, with its old buildings conserving the inimitable flavour of its mediaeval past. Mário Beirão captured the unique nature of this area in these fine verses:

Esta Alfama, de Paços quinhentistas,
Que ostentam naus — brasões do mar ovante,
Nos seus cunhais — confusa, alucinante

De ruelas, sombras, coisas imprevistas;
Sonha rotas no Oceano; áureas conquistas;
Reinos estranhos, lá, no mais distante
Dos horizontes; plagas do Levante;
Auroras como lumes de ametistas!

A variety of colours are freely splashed onto the whiteness of the buildings. Here and there, through the labyrinthine area of Alfama are unbelievably narrow steep winding streets crisscrossing and laden with poetic mystery and reminiscences of past splendour; these streets vibrate with renewed vigour when the traditional festivities of the Popular Saints are celebrated in the month of June.

The popular Rossio railway station.

ROSSIO SQUARE

A splendid... large, beautiful, and well planned square, according to Tirso de Molina's just description of it, wherein all the history and all the dynamic present of Lisbon are concentrated, with the statue of Pedro IV, the first constitucional king of Portugal in the centre, dominating from his pedestal the front of the National Theatre and the church of São Domingos, the largest in Lisbon whose only nave is held up by lovely pink marble columns.

Rossio Square, with its fountains, florists, kiosks — where you can buy any European newspaper —, its cafés and curious railway station close by, is a genuinely stimulating human scene. In Rossio everything is movement, everything seems to be imbued with the incontrollable desire to live freely, to breathe deep of the most intense vital aromas. Swarms of people are constantly going from one side to another. Everyone looks and is looked at — but here the looks are not offensive, they merely seem to greet us in a friendly fashion throughout the length and breadth of this delightful district of Rossio, the only part of Lisbon destroyed by the 1755 earthquake that was not rebuilt, and therefore still largely preserving its pre-Pombalian appearance.

It was right here in the area of the Rossio Square where the aristocrats living in St. George's Castle, the merchants established in the environs of the port, and the common people first began to live together

Flower stalls in Rossio Square.

Rossio Square and the Dona Maria II Theatre.

democratically. Before being built up, O Rossio was a plot of land where cattle markets and horse races were held; it was also used for pig killings. This open space in the city became so popular with the people of Lisbon that in the XIII century, when the king Don Dinis wanted to build slaughter houses and shops there, the municipality took the monarch to court and revindicated the rights of the people to have Rossio continue being an open space.

The history of the square is identified with that of the city, both regarding daily customs and important events. In former times, the high class citizens of Lisbon watered their horses in O Rossio, looked longingly at the girls walking by, and commented on the latest court stories and gossip.

One turbulent night, when the population of Lisbon mutinied, the Mestre de Aviz was acclaimed as king in Rossio Square. Another historic event that took place in O Rossio was on Easter Day in 1506 when a terrible slaughter lasting three days took place, resulting in the death of two thousand Jews and heretics.

The Palace of the Inquisition formerly stood in the square on the same spot as the present site of the theatre whose first director was the famous Portuguese playwright Gil Vicente.

In the pink palace beside the Municipal Theatre a historic conspiracy of Portuguese nobles took place on December 1st 1640, which led to the country's independence from Spain. O Rossio was always, throughout the ages, the centre for all types of

Figueira Square, with St. George's Castle in the background.

political conspiracies, sometimes against the monarchy, others against the Republic, and later against Salazar.

The real name of Rossio Square is Pedro IV, the king whose statue stands in its centre with a gesture offering the people of Lisbon a liberal constituion drawn up and developed in Brazil. But the will of the people has irrevocably named the square Rossio, and everyone knows and calls it by this name.

FIGUEIRA SQUARE

This is situated beside the Rossio Square and is surrounded by streets full of bars and popular restaurants where the delicious wines of the country are drunk and also a high quality old brandy. The atmosphere of Figueira Square is not bustling and dynamic like O Rossio. It is calmer here, but the popular and the historical are also inextricably intermingled. In the centre of Figueira Square stands the equestrian statue of Don João I, and from the opposite corner to the castle, the unmistakable pile of St. George's castle can be seen on the horizon.

LISBON'S FOLKLORE

Among the rich and evocative folklore of Lisbon, the *fado* occupies the most outstanding place. This is an essentially sentimental song, the lyrical expression of the Portuguese soul, mingled with feelings of fatality,

Two fado *singers performing.*

sadness and hope, deriving, according to some authors from the mediaeval Portuguese songs and Mozarabic *jaryas.* In the delightful cadence of the *fado* both nostalgia for the past and laments for an adverse present are to be found.

The *fado* became popular in the XIX century with the *cantadeiras,* with their black dresses and black shawls, and the *cantadores,* accompanied by the melancholy notes of violas and guitars, and they began to perform in the typical cafés in the Bairro Alto and Alfama.

Another singular theme of Lisbon's folklore is the celebration of the «Feira da Ladra» where they sell everything — from the seemingly most useless of objects to the valuable work of art, including new and old clothes, shoes, pottery, books... It is a colourful scene, described in verse by Henrique O'Neill during the last century:

> Salve, três vezes, venerável feira!
> Derradeiro degrau que o artefacto,
> Cumprindo a lei inexorável, cega,
> Que impérios, tribos, monumentos, choças,
> Astros, boninas condenou à morte,
> Desce para voltar a ser mesquinha
> Matéria-prima de futuras obras!

The feast days of the «Popular Saints» (St. John, St. Anthony, and St. Peter) that take place in the month of June in the Alfama district, also offer an extraordinarily dynamic spectacle that leaves an indelible memory.

And the precinct of the «Feira Popular» must of course not be left out, with its bars — among them the «Café dos Pretos» particularly outstanding for its exquisite coffee and the originality of its African décor, — its grilled sardines eaten in the open, its chickens cooked on spits, its restaurants of every sort, its festive spirit, gaiety and overflowing vitality that enlivens the summer nights in Lisbon.

Four scenes representing Portugal's rich and picturesque folklore.

A view of the palace where the Marquis de Pombal was born.

THE ANCIENT ART MUSEUM

This is Portugal's most important museum, installed in a magnificent palace not far from the Tagus and close to the former Royal Palace. Among the main pictorial works in this museum or, the «Museum with the Green Windows» as it is also called, are: *The Temptation of St. Anthony,* one of Hieronymus Bosch's most famous paintings; *The Fountain of Life* by Holbein; *St. Jerome* by Dürer, paintings by Veláz-quez who was of Portuguese descent, and Ribera, and the fine collection of Portuguese primitives, especially the excellent panels of Nuno Gonçalves making up the famous *Polyptic of St. Vincent,* an interesting allegory in paint in which soldiers, merchants, friars, townsfolk, knights and princes sur-round the Patron Saint of Lisbon in a varied multitude, among them being the Infante Don Henrique the Navigator.

Other works of interest are: the richly decorated monstrance worked in gold brought from Quíloa by Gil Vicente, altar-pieces from different convents in the country, silver plates — the finest in Europe — and other jewels; also collections of pottery and tapestries. Also worthy of mention are the many sculptures enriching the artistic content of the museum.

The Ancient Art Museum is situated in the Rua das Janelas Verdes, which means the Street of the Green Windows, a name that reminds one of the poem by José Newton entitled *«De uma janela de Lisboa, em manhã de Maio».*

An impressive view of the Gothic ruins of the church in the convent do Carmo.

A view of the Luís de Camões Square.

The Temptations of St. Anthony, *a work by Hieronymus*
Bosch on show in the Ancient Art Museum.

The Polyptich of the Infante, *by Nuno Gonçalves.*

St. Jerome, *a work by Albrecht Dürer, part of the*
collection in the Ancient Art Museum.

A partial view of the port and the Maritime Terminal of Lisbon.

THE PORT

Lisbon has one of the most important ports in the world, a vital centre for sea communications between Europe, Africa, and America. The quays, dykes and goods warehouses in the port of Lisbon cover a surface area of no less than two million square metres. The port, stretching out from the strand forms an estuary of colossal dimensions.

From the Santa Catarina vantage point a vast impressive panoramic view comprising the Tagus, the quaysides and the port of Lisbon can be seen. The view from high up on the 25th of April Bridge is equally grandiose.

To go down to the port of Lisbon from the steep little

River port, the «April 25th» bridge and a monument to Christ the King in the background.

streets in of A Bica district is a most unique sight. Irregular steps appear everywhere and the Tagus estuary is like some fabulous kaleidoscope. Down below, the river scene is filled with cranes, masts and sails and looks to be magically ruffled on the surface of the water by the foam whipped up by the breeze blowing gently round the port. It could almost be said to be the same mythological wind that caressed Ulysses' forehead when he created the city of Lisbon on the banks of the Tagus, described by Armando Ventura Ferreira in these words:

Mito grego
ou das Tágides nascida
cidade nossa onde a solidão não pesa

porque duma colina se vê a outra
aqui deixou a Grécia um raio de imaginação...

In the streets close by the port are many bars, beer houses, sea food bars, restaurants and night clubs. The atmosphere is cosmopolitan and popular as well, flavoured with typical elements around the Duque da Terceira Square where the statue of the Liberator of Lisbon stands in the centre, seeming to control the busy coming and going of the picturesque trams and the bustling streets of Bernardino Costa, Alecrim, Remolares and Nova do Carvalho.
The port of Lisbon is one the great attractions of the city which one XIX century Portuguese poet, João de Lemos, called: *Princesa dos vastos mares.*

The Spanish tapestry
room in the National
Palace at Ajuda.

A view of the Dance Hall.

The chamber in which
Don João IV was
crowned king in the
National Palace at Ajuda.

A view of the Carriage Museum.

One of the carriages in the Museum.

The Don Afonso de Alburquerque Square, the Palace of Belém and the changing of the guard.

THE CARRIAGE MUSEUM

Situated in the Afonso de Alburquerque Square — Belém —, is the most varied collection of old carriages that the most demanding enthusiast could ever dream of. The vehicles, among them the most outstanding being the luxury coaches used in the XVII, XVIII and XIX centuries, are pleasant to look at, their elegance magically erasing any feeling of anachronism. The principle carriages of the former Portuguese court are here in the museum, the one that belonged to Filipe II (Filipe I of Portugal) remarkable for its originality and for being the oldest in the collection, and João V's carriage being the most imposing and luxurious.

Two views of the monastery of the Jerónimos.

The doorway of the church of the Jerónimos. ▷

THE HIERONYMITES

The monastery and church of the Hieronymites (Os Jerónimos) — true marvels of Portuguese Renaissance art —, were built at the beginning of the XVI century on the same spot as where the altar erected in honour of Our Lady of the Navigators was formerly situated, before which Vasco da Gama passed in prayer the whole night previous to his departure on the historic voyage to India. This was the dawn of the prodigious Portuguese Empire when the grandeur of its capital inspired André Falção de Resende, a XVI century poet, to write this impressive but nevertheless justified panegyric:

A partial view of the elegant cloister of the Jerónimos.

*É Lisboa um mar profundo
De vária navegação;
É um compêndio do mundo,
Aonde tudo acharão;
Asia, África, Europa,
Nova terra, Mundo novo;
Comércio, nobreza, povo,
Tudo anda a vento em popa.*

The wealth brought by Vasco da Gama from the lands he discovered were for the most part devoted to the building of the fine edifice of the Hieronymites. Miraculously spared from the devastation of the 1755 earthquake, it is the most valuable and representative monument of the Manueline period. Both Gothic and Renaissance styles live in harmony in the Hieronymites. The winged beauty of the great southern door of the church facing the Tagus forcibly commands our attention, as does the portal on the side of the bridge with its genuine architectural filigree work, the vault with its elegant pillars, and the decorative cloister. Altogether, such exuberant artistic wealth gives the impression of a successful and markedly personal work of art.

Among the tombs inside the nave, the most outstanding are those of Vasco da Gama and Camões, the latter empty since 1755, the year when the terrible earthquake caused the ashes of the poetic genius of *Os Lusíadas* to be scattered to the four winds.

From the south portico of the church of the Jerónimos not long ago, a popular procession of cod fishermen used to leave once every year to invoke the

A corner of the Jerónimos' cloister.

One of the rooms in the Ethnological Museum.

Two views and the west door of the monastery of the Jerónimos.

Part of the cloister of the Jerónimos.

protection of the Virgin before setting forth on their ocean voyage.

The inside of the church is lit up by sunlight just as if its walls were miraculously transparent. The light comes from the high dome which pours daylight into the interior of the church of the Jerónimos whose columns have a romantic pallour comparable to that of stalagmites.

Vasco da Gama and his sailors, when preparing to set off on their adventure to the far-off lands that were to become part of the Portuguese empire, one of the lar-

gest in the world, after paying their respects to the king, went to bow before the statue of Our Lady of the Jerónimos to ask for good fortune to accompany them on their travels. A Portuguese poet who lived between the XIX and XX centuries, Luís do Magalhães, wrote this fine sonnet entitled *O ex-voto do templo dos Jerónimos:*

À beira d'água, esplêndido, a alvejar,
Do Venturoso o Templo rendilhado,
Na saudade do homérico passado,
Olha, nostálgico e em silêncio, o Mar.

A Viagem triunfal a remembrar,
Do Mar nasceu, ao Mar consagrado,

Todo de cordas náuticas ornado,
Como nau aprestada a navegar.

Abrindo, ao alto, em leque, os seus pilares
Evocam indostânicos palmares,
Terras das nossas colossais Ilíadas.

E, como en sonho, na visão marmórea,
Escuto a Fé cantando a nossa glória
Num outro poema, gémeo dos «Lusíadas».

Art and history meet in this church which is from every point of view one of the city of Lisbon's most interesting monuments.

THE ETHNOLOGICAL MUSEUM

Situated in the Praça do Império and founded in 1817 by the erudite researcher doctor Leite de Vasconcelos, the Ethnological Museum houses several collection of items of extraordinary archaeological value. Its valuable contents include exhibits from the lower paleolithic period to the Middle Ages, and is of great interest to the visitor.

A mosaic on show in the Ethnological Museum.

The hydroplane Santa Cruz kept in the Naval Museum.

A model of the ship used by the Portuguese discoverers in the XVI and XVII centuries.

A night time view of the illuminated fountain opposite the monastery of the Jerónimos.

THE NAVAL MUSEUM

This is the most modern museum in Lisbon and also stands in the Praça do Império. The museum houses some interesting collections of caravels, boats, and all types of Portuguese sailing vessels, along with models of ships, artillery pieces, weapons, uniforms, and every type of naval instrument from different periods.

The collection of royal galleons is worthy of special mention, as is the sextant invented by Gago Coutinho and the first hydroplane in which the latter and his companion Sacadura Cabral crossed the Atlantic by air for the first time.

The Naval Museum is situated in one of the most attractive spots in the city, in a very well looked after area with a wide modern structure, to which the presence of the lovely church of the Jerónimos and the proximity of the Torre de Belém lend a historical and artistic prestige. In the rooms of this museum the enterprising Portuguese spirit is ever present, and when contemplating these old ships, cannon, and different naval weapons, it is not difficult to evoke the prodigious courage that inspired the Portuguese, the inhabitants of a small but admirable country, to discover and conquer vast lands situated thousands of miles from the coasts of Portugal, and to create an empire of an impressive size and to keep it tenaciously for centuries, until the XX century in fact. A visit to the Naval Museum in Lisbon is to have an ideal view of the greatness of an illustrious people who succeeded in going down in history with a glorious name thanks to their own efforts.

A view of the Torre de Belém.

THE BETHLEHEM TOWER

Built between the years 1515 and 1521, the Bethlehem Tower, a fortress overlooking the Tagus estuary, is one of the most chracteristic monuments of the splendid Manueline period. In the decoration of its elegant tower the most diverse elements representing the navigating spirit of the Portuguese people can be seen, and the building constitutes the symbolic essence of the reign of Don Manuel the Fortunate.

It is the balanced proportion of the architectural line that is most impressive in this building, designed by the great artist Francisco de Arruda. The severe military design of the outside in perfect harmony with the subtle grace of the interior Gothic precinct. The Bethlehem Tower whose battlements formerly arose right by the Tagus, is one of the most endearingly characteristic views in Lisbon and a place much frequented by tourists. The old fortress has preserved all the grace of its Moorish domes, its lovely balconies and, most of all, that poetic aura of the past emanating from this unique white-walled domain. The Lisbon of the Torre de Belém is what Antonio Nobre writes about:

> *Lisboa à beira-mar, cheia de vistas (...)*
> *Ó Lisboa dos líricos pregões...*
> *Lisboa com o Tejo das Conquistas,*
> *Mais os ossos prováveis de Camões!*
> *Ó Lisboa de mármore, Lisboa!*

A monument to the discoveries and to the Infante Don Henrique (Prince Henry the Navigator) in Belém.

A partial view of the city from the vantage point of São Pedro de Alcântara.

A statue to the Marquis de Pombal. ▷

VANTAGE POINTS IN LISBON

Lisbon is a city of many vantage points. It could be said that the city, enchanted by her own beauty takes pleasure in looking at herself in leisurely fashion from any one of the strategically placed look-out positions reflecting her image, so well described by Oliva Guerra in *Lisboa do Encantamento:*

> *Lisboa... Céu azul, outeiros altos,*
> *Berço de luz sobre o mar*
> *A embalar*
> *Sobre um pedestal firme de granito...*
> *Grande janela aberta*
> *Sobre os confins do Infinito...*

> *Princesa enfeitiçada*
> *Que ao nascer, numa hora ainda incerta,*
> *Por influxos divinos,*
> *Foste fadada*
> *Para largos, esplêndidos destinos...*

From the look-out on St. George's Castle there is a vast panoramic view of great beauty, delightfully set out at different levels: São Vicente, the cathedral, the Mouraria district with its charming mediaeval structures, the Praça do Comércio, Rossio, on one side, and on the other, Graça, the Monte de São Gens, the Penha de França, Santa Catarina, O Carmo, the church of São Roque, Campolide, Almada, the Ribatejo meadows...

The aqueduct das Águas
Livres, the small chapel
of St. Jerome and a view
of the Estufa Fria.

Two partial views of the
Estufa Fria.

A view of one of Lisbon's picturesque lifts

The outside of the bull ring do Campo Pequeno in Lisbon, and two scenes from a bullfight in which it is forbidden to kill the bull.

Another splendid vantage point is the one on São Pedro de Alcântara near to the Bairro Alto which overlooks the northern and eastern part of Lisbon, with the smart Avenida da Liberdade at its feet.

There are further wonderful views to be seen from the look-outs on Santa Luzia close to St. George's Castle and in the Alfama district, Monsanto, Senhora do Monte and Santa Catarina, and in general, from any of the seventeen high points overlooking the city.

ESTUFA FRIA

Built in 1910, the Estufa Fria is situated high up in the Edward VII park. The designer of the project, Raúl Carapinha — a famous Portuguese architect and painter —, used the hollow in a rock found in the locality for the construction of the Estufa Fria. Extended in 1926, A Estufa was officially inaugurated in 1930. Later on, a covered theatre building on soberly elegant lines was built on the highest point in the garden where musical shows, dances, theatrical performances and the like took place.

In the Estufa Fria the loveliest and most varied botanical species from Portugal and from tropical countries grow in a wonderful natural framework. It is a real paradise and a haven of peace and tranquility, a genuine poetic oasis of vegetation in the centre of the city.

This marvellous garden — a truly ideal spot — is protected from the outside by an original system of walls and beamed roofs which by sheltering it from the rigours of winter and summer, keep the atmosphere at a temperature devoid of sudden changes. The name Estufa Fria is derived from this fact.

The jungle-like aspect of the garden is certainly fascinating with its zigzagging paths, shady groves, bright pools, splashing waterfalls, rustic steps, poetic grottos, miniature bridges, and all this together with hidden corners which look like rooms covered by Nature with the purpose of giving shelter to Eros.

THE BULLS

This spectacle is deeply-rooted in Portugal, especially in Ribatejo, but differs from the Spanish bull fight in that it is not permitted to kill the bull. Nevertheless, the struggle between man and bull offers a great deal of excitement and brilliance in the Portuguese arenas. For bull-fighting on horse back, the gentlemen are dressed in XVIII century costume as it was then when the great bull-fights became accepted in Portugal.

The picturesque spectacle begins when the horsemen, «bandarilheiros» (dart placers) and «forcados» come into the arena. The members of the group («quadrilha») stand in front of the presidential box and greet the authorities. Then the horsemen, tricorn in hand, go from right to left saluting the public and performing to music various exercises of the Portuguese bull-fighting school.
The Lisbon bull-ring in Hispano-Arab style is situated in Campo Pequeno, beside the Avenida da República, and covers an area of 5.000 sq. metres.

The Swan Lake in the Campo Grande Garden.

Two views of the Avenida dos Estados Unidos and the Saldanha Square, with the Avenida da República. ▷

The chamber of the Infante Don Henrique (Prince Henry the Navigator) in the Military Museum.

THE MILITARY MUSEUM

Standing in the Largo do Museo de Artilharia, and founded in 1842, this is a most interesting museum which houses valuable collections of paintings and sculpture, besides several pieces of artillery from different periods. Also of note is the collection of military uniforms used by Portuguese soldiers in the African campaigns, the war against Napoleon, and in the civil strife of the XIX century. The different rooms in the Military Museum are specially designed to house the items making up the various collections, and all of these give us a historical reflection of the development of military institutions in Portugal.

In a way it can be said that it is here in the Military Museum where the patriotic spirit of the Portuguese nation is symbolically present, this admirable spirit that Camões wrote about in *Os Lusíadas,* and also Gil Vicente in the following verse:

> *Cobrai fama de ferozes,*
> *Não de ricos, que é perigosa!*
> *Dourai a pátria vossa*
> *con mais nozes que vozes.*
> *Avante, avante, Lisboa!*

A view of the Vasco da Gama chamber.

The Don José I chamber in the Military Museum.

THE CHURCH OF THE MOTHER OF GOD

Formerly belonging to the convent founded in 1509 by queen Dona Leonor, widow of João II and sister of the king Don Manuel I, it was later restored by João III. It is one of the most successful and evocative samples of religious architecture of the Manuelin period, an outstanding age in the urban development of Lisbon. The church of the Mother of God has a fine Manuelin style portico bearing the escutcheons of João II and Dona Leonor. The Renaissance style cloister is worthy of special mention with its interesting collection of old tiles in various original colours.

The church was badly damaged as a result of the earthquake that devastated Lisbon in 1755 and was one of the buildings trapped between the city walls. The façade was not recovered until 1873, but was then restored on the lines of the model painted by Gregório Lopes in his famous triptych, now in the Museum of Ancient Art.

Inside the church the large XVIII century nave is particularly outstanding. The chapel of the church is interesting and in it are kept some valuable paintings by

The façade of the church of the
Mother of God.

Interior of the church of the Mother of
God.

The choir in the church of the Mother of God.

primitive Portuguese artists and several relics, among them those of St. Ann, martyred in Cologne together with St. Gertrude and her 11.000 companions. Gregório Lopes painted the history of St. Ann and the arrival of her relics at Xabregas, and Maximilian of Austria offered these to queen Leonor when she founded the convent of the Mother of God. The walls of the lower choir — the original chapel was built in the time of Dona Leoncr —, are decorated with XVI century tiles from Seville and inside there is a XVIII century reliquary. In the sacristy which dates from the middle of the XVII century, there are some XVI century paintings and several canvases by Gonçalves, a XVIII century painter.

The church of the Mother of God is associated with the far-reaching transformation of the Portuguese capital brought about in the reign of Don Manuel I, and constitutes, in spite of having been restored, one of the most representative buildings of that splendid period of Portugal's history. Lisbon, at that time, was the capital of a great empire whose power was increasing and which practically covered the entire globe. Only two great monuments were left intact by the 1755 earthquake from Lisbon's outstanding Manuelin edifices, these were the Jerónimos and the Torre de Belém. But the church of the Mother of God which was only partially saved, contributes with its presence, to an evocation of the greatness of the Lisbon that was damaged by the earthquake in the middle of the XVIII century.

THE CITY MUSEUM

This museum is provisionally installed in the elegant Palace da Mitra in Marvila, a former episcopal residence. In the entrance courtyard there is a tomb dating from Roman times. The valuable contents of the City Museum allow a re-creation of Lisbon's history and urban development to be made.

The collections of paintings, engravings, and documents related to the city are most interesting, especially those dating from the XVII to the XIX century. The ethnographic collection is also noteworthy.

THE BASÍLICA DA ESTRELA

Also known as the Basilica of the Heart of Jesus, building on it was begun in 1779 on the initiative of Dona Maria I, the wife of the king consort Pedro III after a vow she made if she bore a child. The architects in charge of the enterprise were Mateus Vicente and Manuel Roynaldos whose inspiration was based on the architectural lines of the convent at Mafra.

The façade of the Estrela Basilica consists of two towers and a high dome (cimborium) and has

A view of the Alfama district, a bas-relief kept in the City Museum.

allegorical figures and statues of saints worked by Machado de Castro. The inside of the church is richly decorated and on the high altar there is a picture depicting the heart of Jesus.

The body of Santo Expério can be seen in a crystal coffin; this formerly lay in the Roman catacombs and was given to Portugal as a present by Pius VI in 1791. Also of interest is the tomb of Queen Maria with its Latin inscriptions.

The Basílica da Estrela is a fine vantage point from which to contemplate the splendid panoramic view of Lisbon stretching out towards the Tagus.

The lake in the garden da Estrela, and a view of the Basílica da Estrela.

The façade of the Câmara Municipal Palace.

A view of the magnificent Salão Nobre.

The Islamic Art Gallery in the Gulbenkian Museum.

The gilded silver mask of an Egyptian mummy. ▷

THE GULBENKIAN MUSEUM

Created from the valuable bequest of Calouste Gulbenkian, the museum was opened to the public in 1969. Housed in an ultramodern building on the Avenida de Berna, it has an important collection of objects of the most diverse nature. The most interesting of these collections are those consisting of ivories and Arab, Mediaeval, Chinese and Japanese pieces, a collection of French painting and another of sculpture. Among the most noteworthy paintings in the Gulbenkian Museum are: *Portrait of an Old Man* by Rembrandt, *Portrait of Helena Fourment* by Rubens, and *The Man and the Doll* by Degas.

Also fascinating are the collections of XVIII and XIX century silver pieces, and the large amount of valuable Regency, Louis XV and Louis XVI style furniture.

The collection housed in this important Lisbon museum is made up of the magnificent art collections amassed by Calouste Gulbenkian throughout forty fruitful years. Objects from these different collections are rationally set out in the rooms of the museum, and belong to periods dating from 2,800 years before Christ, to the XX century.

In order that the visitor might have a full appreciation of the museum, it consists of two circuits. One, devoted to Oriental Art collections with original works from Egypt, Syria, the Islamic Orient, and the Far

The auditorium in the Gulbenkian Foundation.　　　　　　　*A Persian prayer niche dating from the XIII century.* ▷

East. In this circuit, there are also collections of Greco-Roman items.

Along the second circuit, European works of art can be seen, among which the collections of paintings, sculpture, tapestries, jewels, ivory, glass, coins, and furniture are of note.

The Gulbenkian Museum also has a fine library, exhibition gallery and large lecture halls.

The Foundation created by Calouste Gulbenkian at number 45 Avenida de Berna, publishes two important magazines: Colóquio/Artes and Colóquio/Letras. The first, published five times per year is beautifully printed on embossed paper and illustrated with artistic reproductions in black and white and colour. Its pages contain work by reputed international specialists on the subjects of painting, sculpture, music, the cinema, and engraving, with a lengthy final section where the most important artistic events on the international scene are commented on.

The other magazine, Colóquio/Letras, is also well produced and important Portuguese intellectuals and writers contribute to it, along with writers from other countries. It publishes essays, stories, poems, and works of literary criticism. This magazine devotes special attention to Portuguese and Brazilian letters, but is also open to literary trends from France, Spain, Italy, Poland, and other countries.

Both the Museum and the publications by the Calouste Gulbenkian Foundation are a splendid example of the art and culture of Portugal.

The façade of the Palace das Necessidades.

THE PALACE OF AS NECESSIDADES

This former royal palace was built between 1745 and 1750 on the orders of king Don João V. The architect Caetano Tomás de Sousa directed work on the building. This was the official residence of the kings of Portugal until, with the departure of Don Manuel II in 1910, the monarchy in Portugal was abolished. Now, the Palace of As Necessidades is the seat of the Foreign Ministry. Of particular note are the magnificent gardens surrounding the palace which contain a varied collection of exotic plants. The works of art that formerly decorated the interior of the Palace of As Necessidades are now distributed around different museums in Portugal and in the palaces of Ajuda, Queluz, and Sintra.

The building stands in the street of the same name, and in the centre there is a fountain dating from 1747, in the shape of an obelisk.

Not far from the Palace of As Necessidades is the church of St. Francis de Paula where the tomb of Mariana Vitória, the wife of José I, lies.

The façade of the National Assembly Palace.

THE NATIONAL ASSEMBLY

This building was formerly occupied by the convent of São Bento. At the end of the XIX century it was completely restored under the direction of the architect Ventura Terra in order to install the dependencies of the legislative chambers there. It was again restored in 1935.

The Palace of the National Assembly has a sumptuous façade and a beautifully proportioned staircase leads up to it. Outstanding features inside the building are the Sala dos Passos Perdidos, decorated by João Vaz e Columbano who painted several portraits depicting well-known figures in Portuguese politics, and the Sala das Sessões, a wide lecture theatre of fine proportions decorated with paintings and sculptures. The palace also houses the National Archives of a Torre do Tombo, a valuable collection consisting of the Book of Hours of don Duarte, dating from the XV century, a XVI century bible, 60 illustrated manuscripts of *Leitura Nova,* among other important works.

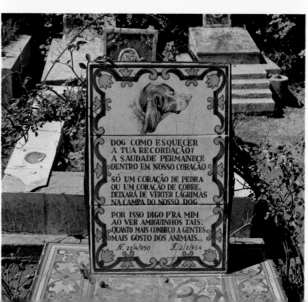

DOG COMO ESQUECER
A TUA RECORDAÇÃO?
A SAUDADE PERMANECE
DENTRO EM NOSSO CORAÇÃO

SÓ UM CORAÇÃO DE PEDRA
OU UM CORAÇÃO DE COBRE,
DEIXARÁ DE VERTER LÁGRIMAS
NA CAMPA DO NOSSO DOG

POR ISSO DIGO P'RA MIM
AO VER AMIGUINHOS TAIS:
QUANTO MAIS CONHEÇO A GENTES
MAIS GOSTO DOS ANIMAIS...

N. 21/4/1950   F. 2/1/1954

*Several
views of the
Zoological
Garden with
some of its
inhabitants.*

A close-up of the Illuminated Fountain.

THE ZOOLOGICAL GARDEN

Situated in Palhavã, this Zoo is undoubtedly one of the most outstanding of its type. It stands not far from the Instituto de Oncologia in the Quinta das Laranjeiras, a lovely estate that used to belong to the count of Farrobo and is now owned by the state. The Avenida de Berna is near by and the Parque de Palhavã is close to it; in this park stands the palace built by the count of Sarzedas in the middle of the XVII century where queen Maria Francisca of Savoy died in 1683, and which is now the seat of the Calouste Gulbenkian Foundation.

The Zoo has a fine collection of the most varied types of animals from the most distant lands and from all the climates under the sun. Lisbon's Zoo is one of the most complete and fascinating in the whole of Europe. Lions, hippopotamus, monkeys of different species, and many other animals live in this vast Zoological Garden.

Another interesting feature of this garden is the collection of floral species from every country, among these the marvellous specimens in the lovely rose garden are particularly outstanding.

Some seven kilometres from the Zoological Garden is the Benfica residential area, also with some fine plants. In the São Domingos Square stand the church of the convent of the same name where the Viceroy of India, Don João de Castro und Don João das Regras lie buried.

Three views of the animated popular fair held in the Amusement Park where thousands of people go from stall to stall enjoying the happy atmosphere of the fairground.

Two view of Lisbon's International Fair.

CUISINE

Lisbon is a city where you can eat extremely well and at reasonable prices. Cod is the Portuguese dish par excellence. It must be added that the cod is always top quality, being specially cured to give it an unmistakably pleasant taste. It is usually eaten cooked along with potatoes and oil and roasted with potatoes, onions, garlic and olives in its more authentic version. White wine (vinho verde branco) goes excellently with both methods of cooking cod.

Another important dish in Lisbon's gastronomic repertoire is Portuguese stew, with chicken, beef, *enchidos* sausage, pork, potatoes, cabbage, green beans and rice. An old local red wine goes extremely well with this succulent baroque dish.

Iscas constitute another typical dish of the Lisbon area, this includes liver — cut into fine slices and macerated in white wine and vinegar — fried with melt and garnished with boiled potatoes.

The exquisite sardines, grilled and accompanied by boiled potatoes are popular in Lisbon where there is also fish of the quality of red mullet, sole, hake, and the most varied and tasty shell-fish including crab and lobster, barnacles, cockles, scampi and prawns.

The local cheeses — fresh or aged — and the magnificent fruit of Portugal are the best dessert.

As for wines, both red and white, young and mature, are, in this country, always excellent and not too strong, with a delicious friendly palate.

Fruit, cheeses, sweets... to satisfy the most demanding of palates.

A wide range of exquisite shell-fish, taken with the typical «vinho verde».

The frango na púcara, *chicken stew, is one of the tastiest dishes of the typical cuisine.*

Two partial views of Estoril.

ESTORIL

Estoril is where the so-called Portuguese *riviera* really begins. This is a first class tourist centre with modern hotels, swimming pools, golf courses, tennis courts, riding schools, a sailing club and amenities for every type of sport.

But among the many tourist attractions to be found in Estoril are, during the day, its wonderful beaches, and at night, its famous Casino standing on the highest point in the Park, offering in addition to other amusements, gaming rooms where one can try one's luck at roulette or Bacarat. Estoril has a mild climate and some truly delightful countryside.

The Palmela Palace and the Guía lighthouse at Cascais.

CASCAIS

A former fishing village some three kilometres from Estoril, Cascais is now one of Portugal's most flourishing tourist resorts. The citadel of Cascais was the summer residence of the kings of Portugal from 1871 to 1910. Beside its walls stretches the Passeio de Santo António, with two superimposed terraces fringed by elegant palm trees.

Situated in the so-called Portuguese Costa do Sol in an impressive bay, Cascais has some excellent hotels and restaurants. Several houses surrounded by lovely gardens dating from the time when the court spent the summers in Cascais are still preserved.

The National Palace at Sintra.

SINTRA

Overlooking the majestic mountain range that bears its name whose magnificent vegetation Byron described as «glorious Eden» in his poem *Childe Harold,* Sintra with its fantastic park, its two royal palaces, and its ancient Castelo dos Mouros, is one of the loveliest romantic scenes imaginable. Its delightful personality and the incomparable scenery around it cannot effectively be described. Sintra is something unique, incomparable. It is impossible even to reflect a pale image of its unequalled beauty. Sintra must be seen and its beauty appreciated spiritually to be able to value its charms.

The Royal Palace is outstanding among the monuments at Sintra, this stands in the main square and is a building of definite artistic value. Architecturally, it comprises several styles and was the residence of the kings of Portugal from the XV century. Its illustrious historical past witnessed the voice of Camões reciting the verses of *Os Lusíadas* to the king, and also the laments of Afonso VI the unfortunate monarch whose own brother shut him up in a wing of the palace after taking away his wife and his throne.

The marvellous Parque da Pena, with its steep shaded walks, splashing fountains and century old trees is one of Sintra's greatest attractions. «Today», exclaimed Richard Strauss enthusiastically when he came to Sintra, «is the happiest day of my life! I know Italy, Sicily, Greece, and Egypt, but I have never seen anything like Pena. It's the loveliest thing I've ever seen!»

On top of the Sintra mountains is the Pena Palace — a privileged vantage point from which an impressive mountain top view can be seen, with its curious Dragon gateway, its bell towers and minarettes, its domes with rounded walls, Manueline style windows with capricious Gothic ogives and a fascinating mixture of styles.

There is also a fine view from the mediaeval Castelo dos Mouros, with the blue sea on one side and the convent at Mafra, one of the most majestic monuments in Portugal, on the other.

The entrance to the Pena Palace.

A partial view of the Pena Palace.

The Throne Room in the Queluz Palace.

A partial view of the Queluz Palace.

The Embassadors' Room in the Queluz Palace.

THE NATIONAL PALACE OF QUELUZ

A former royal residence, this magnificent palace is only a few kilometres from Lisbon in the town of Queluz. It is a sumptuous building dating from the second half of the XVIII century, designed by the Portuguese architect Mateus Vicente and the Frenchman Robillon. It has been justifyably referred to as the Portuguese Versailles. The «ceremonial» façade opens onto some beautiful gardens in the style of Versailles. The façade of the royal chamber and the noble sweep of the Lions' staircase are also of interest. Inside the National Palace of Queluz the following are particularly noteworthy: the so-called Casa de Mangas whose walls are decorated with Rato tiles depicting the discoveries made by the Portuguese in different parts of the world; the Reception Gallery — the Embassador's Chamber — whose ceiling has a painting depicting a concert in the court of Don João V and its walls are faced with marble and mirrors; the Council of State Chamber with a painting symbolizing Time on the ceiling, attributed to Pedro Alexandrino; the King's Chamber — also known as the Don Quixote Chamber —, decorated with scenes from «Don Quixote» painted by Manuel da Costa and J. A. Narciso, with a pictorial allegory of the Arts on the ceiling, this room has in it the bed belonging to Pedro IV which is still preserved; the Sala das Merendas with some XVIII century paintings; the Oratory of the princesses Maria José and Maria Doroteia; the Sala de

A panoramic view of the Queluz Palace.

Lanternem, with the portrait of king Don Miguel by Ender; the Music Room with three lovely Venetian crystal candelabra and the ceiling painted in green and pink; then the Throne Room in Louis XV style decorated by José Vicente and Silvestre de Faria.

The Queluz gardens are most interesting, especially the Neptune garden designed by Robillon in the style of Le Nôtre which stretches out through a terrace of archways separated from the park by a balustrade with statues by Manuel Alves and Silvestre de Faria, and the *dos azereiros* garden dating from the time when Marshall Junot installed himself in the palace after Napoleon's troops had invaded Portuguese territory.

SETUBAL

This town, formerly called *Cetobriga,* is situated on the left bank of the mouth of the river Sado and has now become an important industrial city. Also one of the most important fishing ports in the country it has the largest tinning industry in Portugal. There are also prosperous cement and phosphate factories here. Setúbal's main street is the Avenida de Luisa Todi, named after the famous Portuguese singer, which runs parallel to the river and has a park and also the Theatre that goes by the same name nearby, and the Oceanographic Museum with some interesting collections including a particularly fine one of sea sponges.

A partial view of the fishing port and Bocage Square in Setúbal.

Of the monuments to be found in Setúbal, the most noteworthy is the church of Jesus, built at the end of the XV century by the same architect who directed work on the monastery of the Jerónimos. It is a fine example of Gothic architecture with Manuelin style additions. The portico is made from Arrábida marble. Inside, the walls are faced with beautiful XVII century tiles, some with scenes from the life of the Virgin. The Manuelin style cloister is also of interest.

Other churches worthy of mention are those of São Julião, rebuilt at the beginning of the XVI century, and Santa Maria da Graça, dating from the XIII century, rebuilt in the XVI century and beautifully decorated with XVIII century tiles.

Two partial views of Sesimbra.

A fish auction in Sesimbra. ▷

SESIMBRA

An important fishing port and spa, Sesimbra offers the charm of its welcoming nearby beaches and the attraction of the delicious fish to be eaten in its reataurants. The public sale of the fish caught by the fishermen of Sesimbra is a highly picturesque sight. The whole town has kept its delightful image of a small fishing town completely intact.

The parish church is of interest having some XVII century paintings depicting scenes from the popular festivity of Our Lady of the Wounds which has been held on the 3rd and 4th of May since the XVI century.

Contents

LISBON, THE MUCH PRAISED CITY...   2
THE CITY   5
THE CATHEDRAL   10
THE CHURCH OF SANTO ANTÓNIO   13
THE CASA DOS BICOS   14
St. GEORGE'S CASTLE   15
THE TAGUS   17
THE CHURCH OF SÃO VICENTE DE
    FORA   19
THE MUSEUM OF DECORATIVE ARTS   22
THE ALFAMA DISTRICT   26
ROSSIO SQUARE   28
FIGUEIRA SQUARE   31
LISBON'S FOLKLORE   31
THE ANCIENT ART MUSEUM   34
THE PORT   38
THE CARRIAGE MUSEUM   43
THE HIERONYMITES   44
THE ETHNOLOGICAL MUSEUM   51
THE NAVAL MUSEUM   53
THE BETHLEHEM TOWER   54
VANTAGE POINTS IN LISBON   56
ESTUFA FRIA   60
THE BULLS   62
THE MILITARY MUSEUM   64
THE CHURCH OF THE MOTHER OF
    GOD   66
THE CITY MUSEUM   69
THE BASILICA DA ESTRELA   69
THE GULBENKIAN MUSEUM   72
THE PALACE OF AS NECESSIDADES   76
THE NATIONAL ASSEMBLY   77
THE ZOOLOGICAL GARDEN   79
CUISINE   82
ESTORIL   84
CASCAIS   85
SINTRA   86
THE NATIONAL PALACE OF QUELUZ   89
SETUBAL   90
SESIMBRA   92